THE
HONOUR
CODE

'Let Honour always be the plumb-line
of your every action'

PHILLIP VERMEULEN

ISBN: 9798521068463

CONTENTS

Foreword

I have known Apostle Phillip Vermeulen for more than 20 years, and I have had the privilege of working alongside him as both a friend and co-labourer. He is a tremendous grace gift to this generation, and he is passionate about seeing the culture of heaven translated in real tangible terms in the earth. This is evident through the numerous expressions of the Kingdom of God that he has either pioneered or been involved in.

As a friend, I have had occasion to witness first-hand the impact that dishonour has had on him over the years. As a minister of the Gospel, I have had my own personal experiences with it. The flipside is also true; I have seen how authentic honour has released such a tremendous flow of blessing, grace and favour. I am grateful to God that he has given Apostle Phillip the boldness to write this book and bring balance to an often misunderstood and criticised, yet seldomly practiced Biblical principle. There is a tremendous need for the restoration of authentic Biblical honour.

Honour and honouring is often a subject that we shy away from within our post-modernist church culture. This has largely been because of the emergence of cultural superstars within the entertainment, political, business, social, and I daresay, the mainstream church. It has been associated with idolatry and the worship of man. We have demonised honour in the name of humility and have thus lost the tremendous grace and blessing that comes with authentic honouring. One of the first benefits scripture ascribes to honour is longevity (Exodus 20:12)! It is sad that we can have an adage in English that expresses that 'there is even honour amongst thieves', yet the very sound and foundational biblical principle is too often absent in the church and amongst believers.

In this book, The Honour Code, Apostle Phillip gives proper context to honour as a principle, from both a historical, contemporary and scriptural perspective. Here you will find the foundation and precepts that will unlock the rewards that honour brings in the life of the believer; line upon line, precept upon precept. You will learn what authentic honour is, how to apply it in your life, the rewards of honour. You will also learn how to avoid dishonour and what the pitfalls of dishonour are. This timely resource is essential for every believer who is serious about their growth as a believer, and who wants to see the Kingdom of heaven manifested in the earth.

Apostle Howard Pyoos

Senior Leader, Eternal Praise City

South Africa

INTRODUCTION

Thank you for taking the time to read this book. I am genuinely humbled by your support and my heart's desire is to see every life impacted by the truths unpacked here.

I have been in ministry for over two decades now and serve as the founding and senior pastor of MyChurch London. I responded to the call of God at the age of 17. I always served in a local church and submitted to the leadership in that house. My ministry expressions started in the youth department, followed by enrolling full time at Bible College, and then serving on the worship team and sound engineering, and shadowing our senior pastor. After moving to the UK from South Africa, I served again within the youth ministry, worship team, until eventually responding to the call of God to plant churches.

After responding to the call of God to plant churches, my ministry expression was initially pastoral but over the last 10 years, there has been a solidifying of the Prophetic call and in more recent years, the Apostolic call.

To be brutally honest, I can write this book because I have personally experienced the fruit of both dishonour and honour. As a result, I want to bring a holistic understanding to each of you of the principle of honour, the fruit of honour and the purpose of honour according to the Word of God. I don't want anyone else to make the same mistakes and reap the consequences of dishonour.

My heart is to see you walk in a blessing and break-through only God-honour can bring to your life.

The main key I desire to impart to your heart and mind, is that the real power is making the Word of God your own. Let the truths of God's Word transform your thinking and be a measuring stick in all your decision making and the actions you take in life.

Are you ready for an upgrade?

BACKGROUND

Now I know first impressions are that some may find looking at historical accounts a bit boring and tedious, but it is important to understand where we have come from in order to understand better where we are going.

I'd like to start by looking at honour and its role in generations past. One can say honour served as a barometer of virtue and not only highlighted value systems, or lack thereof, but also played a far major role in society than it does today. The value of honour has influenced the moral barometer of society through different eras and impacted how relationships, reputations and religious status were measured. This created an understanding within society of what was right and wrong and in turn informed what was honourable and dishonourable behaviour. Just referencing the writings of Shakespeare, we see that the virtue of honour formed a strong theme in his books, meaning to say that during the times of Shakespeare, honour played a massive role in the culture of the day. If we look at the accounts within the Bible, both Old and New Testament, we see great value placed on honour and honourable men and women of God. I will circle back to take a deeper look at biblical accounts a little later.

Let's start with the period extending from the 14th Century up to the 17th Century. We see a period of time of great reform and also defined historically as different renaissance movements. Accounts have variations but it is generally agreed that the renaissance had its roots in Italy in the 14th century. These reforms in thinking filtered into the rest of Europe over the next two centuries and completely transformed literature, art and religious views, which in turn had a direct impact on Christian renaissance as well.

Renaissance essentially was an increase in humanistic perspectives, which both addressed medieval superstitions as well as brought veins of thought that also addressed authority, traditions and religious controls. The unleashing of new thinking that renaissance brought impacted areas such as political, economic, social, artistic and intellectual rebirth but the ripple effects of renaissance definitely impacted and began an era of redefining the impact and role of church culture at the time. Many agree that philosophy, literature and art were promoted and rediscovered as a result.

The role and influence of the church is intertwined with the history of Western Society during the middle Ages. The Roman Catholic church played a pivotal role from the life to death of a person and was found to be the centre of a village or town, especially during the Middle Ages. We also see the church's role and influence in society was very significant back then (not to say it isn't today). It influenced the political decisions, the financial decisions in some cases, and the morals of the church were also reflected in legal frameworks and judgment systems that were set in place. As a result of this, the moral influence of the church meant that the value of honour was transferred into the fabric of society.

How do we know the church had such a significant impact on culture during these centuries? Let's look at Galileo. In 1623 he coined the metaphor "the two books of nature" in order to get out of a sticky situation where one of his students addressed differences between scientific discoveries and scripture. Here we see that strong correlation between religion and science existed among the academics of that day. Actually, quite a few scientists during the renaissance agreed with this; that God revealed himself in both scripture and science and studying both books enabled one to more fully grasp truth. Even in the art world, Michael-Angelo and others attributed their awe of God for impacting their desire to capture his nature in their works. It is fair to say that during those periods the value of honour was far more significant and held a larger influence in culture than it does today. The renaissance brought an increase in humanistic viewpoints where people became more interested in their current life than in the afterlife. This impacted the Roman Catholic religious strongholds and was a catalyst in the reformation to Protestant fundamentalism, which was a revived interest in the Christian faith.

Since then, we have seen a steady increase in humanism since the 17th century and a steady decline in the importance placed on the value of honour. Honour has not fully disappeared, but it certainly is a more rare quality to find in contemporary culture. If we look at our places of work, our churches, our businesses, even in friendships and extended families, we can see how honour is less prevalent and definitely not a priority in society and culture as it should be.

Don't panic! This book is a positive book. Before I continue, I would love to share some stories of honour with you.

On 26th April 1986 when the nuclear plant Chernobyl was about to explode and create a catastrophe impacting the majority of Europe, two plant workers and a soldier sacrificed their own lives in order to honour the preservation of life by wading in radio active materials to go and turn off a system within the plant.

Another account we can reference is Alfred Vanderbilt, who descended from wealth and opulence. He was on board a ship as a first-class passenger. This ship was about to sink, and Alfred sacrificed his life to save children from the lower class from drowning. He did this by giving up his place on a rescue boat and allowed children to take his place in the rescue process.

There was a soldier named John Robert Fox, who during World War 2 gave his exact location to the American army to bomb the area. There were over a thousand German military around his location. This act of honour and sacrifice enabled the American army the ability to launch a counter attack that would prove successful in weakening the German stronghold.

During my research, it was clear that there is a strong correlation in history regarding honour – where honour and sacrifice seemed synonymous. This does not mean being honourable or operating in honour needs to amount to premature death or self-sacrifice.

Honourable also meant respecting a woman's virtue before marriage. Honour is associated with keeping one's word and promises – which links into modern day "good faith and contract". Honour is considered behaving in a certain manner which does not bring the name of one's family into disrepute. Just by mentioning these, we see a link between honour and marriage, honour and family and finally honour and business. Honour underpinned the fabric of our families and communities.

The concern today is how moral relativism is the logic behind an inversion of value systems such as purity, honour, honesty, tolerance, sensitivity, love and hate. I believe that more than ever, we cannot just sit back and accept the picture that is being painted for us and our children of what others decide is right, wrong and operate within the narratives others share, but we must come back to the Word of God and be sure of what God is saying. We need to be intentional about culture. Culture is the fruit of intention. As believers, we need to be intentional about establishing the right culture within our homes, our churches, our communities and our workplaces.

It would be a crying shame for us to simply recede and lose our way in the political red tape and philosophical confusion regarding contemporary issues. God is an unchanging God. He was God at the creation of man. He was God when David was King. He was God when Jesus walked the earth and He continues to be God today. His word and His promises are unchanging. The expression of His truths may differ culturally from generation to generation but the truth of who He ss and what He requires of us does not alter.

Be thankful we are not alone and not abandoned in the current terrain of the 21st century. God has provided us with great assurances that His purposes cannot and will not be frustrated but we can access everything He has promised, and He is a promise keeping God.

As we continue to journey together in this book, I hope every single argument, every pretence, every lofty thought and opinion that rises up against the knowledge of God, will be torn down and destroyed, and every thought that promotes ourselves over His word would be made captive to Christ.

What Is Honour?

According to Merriam-Webster dictionary, honour can be described as;

- A good name or public esteem
- To regard or treat (someone) with admiration and respect
- To give special recognition
- To live up to or fulfil the terms of a commitment
- To salute with a bow in recognition of honour.

As to the origin of honour, secular sources quote the first known use as being during the 13th century, however as believers we know the scriptures referenced honour long before this time stamp. The word 'honour' is derived from Anglo-French 'onur', and from Latin 'honos' and relates to - honesty, integrity, probity, rectitude, righteousness and uprightness.

Here are some examples and statements of honour:

- When we get married, we promise to love and *honour* each other.
- We were *honoured* with the president's presence.
- We need to find an appropriate way to *honour* those who have sacrificed their lives.
- They have established a charity as a way to *honour* his memory.

- They are accused of failing to *honour* their agreements.

Let's take a look at the Old Testament Hebrew words used to describe "honour".

Kabad pronounced as *(kaw-bad');* or **kabed** pronounced *(kaw-bade')* means heavy, weighty and wealthy as well as to be glorious, full of splendour and honour.

Kabowd pronounced as *(kaw-bode')* identifies with glory, wealth, splendour, tribute and honour ascribed to someone of importance to you.

Yeqar pronounced as *(yek-awr')* meaning to assign worth and value on those that you honour. Honouring those who are wealthy and worthy and honouring precious things or that which is costly to obtain.

Hadar pronounced as *(haw-dawr') means* magnificence, beauty, excellency and glory.

Let's move onto the New Testament Greek Words used to describe "honour."

Atimos pronounced as *(at'-ee-mos)* has the opposite meaning and reflects great dishonour. It also maintains a negative attribute and implies to be unhonoured or dishonoured. To look deeper into this word, we find that it also means to be despised, one without honour and one who is less honourable.

Timao pronounced as *(tim-ah'-o)* means to fix value on something or someone and to revere and to place value upon an individual by price.

Protoklisia pronounced as *(pro-tok-lis-ee'-ah)*, this word intends to mean being first and it also denotes to be a chief (highest, uppermost) in an environment. This is why a principality is always honoured because they are a prototype and a context for others to follow.

It is important to note that the bible was written in the Hebrew language in the Old Testament and in the Greek language in the New Testament. These study of these Hebrew and Greek words help us to find the original intent of the writer and to accurately articulate our points.

The word Kabod is highlighted in the Old Testament of the bible and the word Timao is highlighted in the New testament. These words are used in relation to the honour granted by fellow human beings, though in some cases they are used to describe the honour a person grants God. The depth of the word kabod means to be heavy or weighty. The figurative meaning is 'to give weight to someone.' We can conclude that to honour someone, is to give weight or to grant a person a position of respect and authority in one's life. We have seen honour being given on the basis of position, status, or wealth, however consideration must also be given on the basis of character. We must also recognise that while honour is an internal attitude of respect, courtesy, and reverence, it should be accompanied by corresponding action or even obedience. Outside of this posture, honour is incomplete and remains simply lip service.

The primary root of all honour is derived from God as He is the sovereign king, creator and saviour who display His character as a loving and gracious Father. God the Father has bestowed honour on his Son, Jesus Christ *"that all should honour the Son just as they honour the Father. He who does not honour the Son does not honour the Father who sent Him."* John 5:23 NKJV

> *"In as much as these people draw near with their mouths And honour Me with their lips, But have removed their hearts far from Me, And their fear toward Me is taught by the commandment of men"* Isaiah 29:13 NKJV

God the Father, honoured humanity by sending Jesus Christ to die in our place and purchased us with the blood of Jesus Christ. Honour is even seen from God to us. He paid an expensive price.

> *"For you were bought at a price; therefore glorify God in your body and in your spirit, which are God's."* 1 Corinthians 6:20 NKJV

HONOUR is yours to give.

The onus is on you...
The decision lies with you...

Who to honour... When to honour... What to honour.

THE HONOUR LIST

1. Your parents: father and mother

"Honour your father and your mother, that your days may be long upon the land which the Lord your God is giving you." Exodus 20:12 NKJV

"A son honours his father, a servant *his* master. *If then I am the Father, where is* my *honour? if I am* a Master, *where is* My reverence? *Says the* LORD *of* hosts." Malachi 1:6 NKJV

"He answered and said to them, "Why do you also transgress the commandment of God because of your tradition? For God commanded, saying, 'Honour your father and your mother'; and, 'He who curses father or mother, let him be put to death.' But you say, 'Whoever says to his father or mother, "Whatever profit you might have received from me is a gift *to God"— then he need not honour his father* [a] *or mother.' Thus you have made the* [b] *commandment of God of no effect by your tradition."* Matthew 15:3-9 NKJV

"Children, obey your parents in the Lord, for this is right. "Honour your father and mother," which is the first commandment with promise: "that it may be well with you and you may live long on the earth." Ephesians 6:1-3 NKJV

Honour has the ability to keep you out of the realm of premature death

---

2. Those ordained to serve in spiritual matters

"And you shall make [a]holy garments for Aaron your brother, for glory and for beauty. So you shall speak to all who are gifted artisans, whom I have filled with the spirit of wisdom, that they may make Aaron's garments, to consecrate him, that he may minister to Me as priest."* Exodus 28:2-3 NKJV

"Let the elders who rule well be counted worthy of double honour, especially those who labour in the word and doctrine. For the Scripture says, "You shall not muzzle an ox while it treads out the grain," and, "The labourer is worthy of his wages."* Do not receive an accusation against an elder except from two or three witnesses. Those who are sinning rebuke in the presence of all, that the rest also may fear."* 1 Timothy 5:17-20 NKJV

3. Those who are our elders and elderly

"You shall [a] rise before the grey headed and honour the presence of an old man, and fear your God: I am the LORD."* Leviticus 19:32

4. Those in authority: Kings and Governors

"Then David returned to bless his household. And Michal the daughter of Saul came out to meet David,

and said, "How glorious was the king of Israel today, uncovering himself today in the eyes of the maids of his servants, as one of the base fellows [a] *shamelessly uncovers himself!" So David said to Michal, "It was* before the LORD, *who chose me instead of your father and all his house, to appoint me ruler over the people of the* LORD, *over Israel. Therefore I will play music* before the LORD. *And I will be even more undignified than this, and will be humble in my own sight. But as for the maidservants of whom you have spoken, by them I will be held in honour." Therefore Michal the daughter of Saul had no children to the day of her death."* 2 Samuel 6:20-23 NKJV

"Honour all people. Love the brotherhood. Fear God. *Honour the king."* 1 Peter 2:17

5. Ministers of the Gospel

"The elders[*] who direct the affairs of the church well are worthy of double *honour, especially those whose work is preaching and teaching. For Scripture says, "Do not muzzle an ox while it is treading out the grain,"*[a] and *"The worker deserves his wages."*[b] *do not entertain an accusation against an elder unless two or three witnesses bring it. But those elders who are sinning you are to reprove before everyone, so that the others may take warning."* 1Timothy 5:17-20 NKJV

*Apostles, Prophets, Teachers, Evangelists and Pastors are also considered those worthy of double honour.

"He who receives you receives Me, and he who receives Me receives Him who sent Me. He who receives a prophet in the name of a prophet shall receive a prophet's reward. And he who receives a righteous man in the name of a righteous man shall receive a righteous man's reward. And whoever gives one of these little ones only a cup of cold water in the *name of a disciple, assuredly, I say to you, he shall by no means lose his reward."* Matthew 10:40-42 NKJV

6. Each other

"Be kindly affectionate to one another with brotherly love, in *honour giving preference to one another; not lagging in diligence, fervent in spirit, serving the Lord"* Romans 12:10 NKJV

"Let nothing *be done* through selfish ambition or conceit, but in lowliness of mind let each esteem others better than himself."* Philippians 2:3 NKJV

7. Those we may consider less honourable

"And the eye cannot say to the hand, "I have no need of you"; nor again the head to the feet, "I have no need of you." No, much rather, those members of the body which seem to be weaker are necessary. And those members of the *body, which we think to be less honourable, on these we, bestow greater honour; and our unpreventable parts* have greater modesty, *but our presentable parts* have no need. But God composed the body, having given greater *honour to that part* which lacks it, *that there should be no*

[a] *schism in the body, but that* the members should have the same care for one another. *And if one member suffers, all the members suffer with it;* or if one member is *honoured, all the members rejoice with it."* 1 Corinthians 12:21-26 NKJV

8. Those who are Christ ambassadors

"If anyone inquires about Titus, *he is* my partner and fellow worker concerning you. Or if our brethren *are inquired about, they are messengers* [a] of the churches, the glory of Christ. *Therefore show to them,* [b] *and before the churches, the proof of your love and of our boasting on your behalf."* 2 Corinthians 8:23-24 NKJV

9. Those making significant sacrifices for the kingdom to advance

"Receive him therefore in the Lord with all gladness, and hold such men in esteem; because for the work of Christ he came close to death, [a]*not regarding his life, to supply what was lacking in your service toward me."* Philippians 2:29-30

10. Co-labourers in the kingdom

"And we urge you, brethren, to recognize those who labour among you, and are over you in the Lord and [a] *admonish you, and to esteem them very highly in love for their work's sake. Be at peace among yourselves."* 1 Thessalonians 5:12-13 NKJV

11. Everyone

"*Honour all people.* Love the brotherhood. Fear God. *Honour the king.*" 1 Peter 2:17 NKJV

12. Your Spouse

"*Husbands, likewise, dwell with them* with understanding, giving *honour to the wife, as to the weaker vessel, and as being* heirs together of the grace of life, that your prayers may not be hindered." 1 Peter 3:7 NJKV

"*Nevertheless let each one of you in particular so love his own wife as himself, and let the wife see* that she respects *her* husband." Ephesians 5:33 NKJV

A Life Of Honour

1. God releases Honour

1 Chronicles 29:12 NKJV says "Both riches and honour come from You."

We ascribe value, price, riches, glory and tribute to something we revere and honour. In multiple places throughout scripture, both the old and new testament, we can see God placing honour on His children by purchasing them with His blood from sin and death, by giving them His authority in the earth and by giving them dominion and rulership over the works of His hands. This type of honour can only come from God.

If God in His sovereignty has assigned honour to something or someone, we should place honour in the same way.

2. Doing what is right and what is good

"Then the king said, "What honour or dignity has been bestowed on Mordecai for this?" Esther 6:1-3 NKJV

The noble intentions in our hearts to do what is right and what is essentially good for humanity in the eyes of God never goes unnoticed. We find that whatever works we engage in, we are to do it unto the Lord and in due course, reward and honour comes.

Do not pass on an opportunity to be honourable.

3. Wisdom unlocks honour

"The wise shall inherit glory." *Another verse in Proverbs 23:23 highlights "Buy the truth, and sell it not; also wisdom, and instruction, and understanding."* Proverbs 3:35 NKJV

We are to gain wisdom by ascribing a price to it. Once we've gained this wisdom, this is what will bring honour to our lives. When you chose to place value on godly wisdom, you will see your life flourish in a new and greater way

4. Humility underpins honour

"Before destruction the heart of a man is haughty, And before honour is humility.*"* Proverbs 18:12 NKJV

"By humility and the fear of the LORD *Are* riches and honour and life.*"* Proverbs 22:4 NKJV

The opposite of humility is pride. Pride therefore can be seen as one who is without law and a deviation from the original plan of God. Pride says, "I don't need God, I'm above the law of God. I can do this myself. I can do this better". Humility says, "I need the grace of God to enable me." This enabling power of God through His grace brings elevation and honour because your reliance is on the Lord.

No matter how far you go, or how high, the best quality you can have is to remain teachable. There is always something to learn. On this journey of growing in an understanding of honour, I believe there is always a new dimension of honour to be understood and to begin to walk in. Pride will keep you from accessing all of this.

5. Letting go of all strife

> *"It is* honourable for a man to stop striving."* James 3:16

> *"where strife exists every evil work is found."* Proverbs 20:3 NKJV

Strife always affects our worship and our offering (giving). Worship is an act of honour to God and offerings are a physical act of honour placed on God. Strife has the ability to take that away from you. This is why the avoidance of strife is considered honourable.

My wife and I always use the 'treadmill of strife' as a measuring stick when assessing scenarios and experiences. We ask ourselves, "is there strife? Is there contention? Why could this be? And how can we avoid strife or deal with it in a better way?"

Honour and strife are not meant to be seated at the same table

6. The pursuit of righteousness and love

> *"He who follows righteousness and mercy, Finds life, righteousness, and honour."* Proverbs 21:21 NKJV

We must recognise that the foundation of God's throne is righteousness and justice. There must be an internal desire and an outward posture to pursue righteousness and mercy because these two characteristics of God will unlock honour in your life. This means being intentional about what and who you pursue. The instruction is to consider what you follow. Today that means who do you follow on Twitter, what do you pursue in your private time, where do you sow and invest, and do you value the pursuit of righteousness (right-living) and being just?

7. Embracing and Understanding the fear of the Lord

> *"By humility and* the fear of the LORD *Are* riches and honour and life." Proverbs 22:4 NKJV

We see in other parts of scripture that the fear of the Lord is the beginning of the wisdom of God. Wisdom is one of the attributes of honour and the fear of the Lord. This means that sobriety and maturation is needed in our lives to discern accurately the will of God and to position us accordingly to attract that wisdom of God, which in turn is interpreted as honour.

Fear of the Lord brings wisdom – wisdom brings riches and honour and abundant life.

8. Working for the audience of one (God)

> *"He who speaks from himself seeks his own glory; but He who seeks the glory of the One who sent Him is true, and no unrighteousness is in Him."* John 7:18 NKJV

It's always imperative to check the posture of our hearts in recognition to what we do unto the Lord. Failure to do so results in going through the motions and never attracting the attention of God but rather the approval of man.

It is necessary to ask oneself, "Am I seeking His glory and kingdom, or am I speaking from my own intellect and understanding – what am I promoting?"

9. Leading the Church of God well

> *"Let the elders who rule well be counted worthy of double honour, especially those who labour in the word and doctrine. For the Scripture says, "You shall not muzzle an ox while it treads out the grain," and, "The labourer is* worthy of his wages." Do not receive an accusation against an elder except from two or three witnesses. Those who are sinning rebuke in the presence of all, that the rest also may fear." 1 Timothy 5:17-20

We see here that there is an instruction to doubly honour those who deal with preaching and teaching of the Word of God. There is also a dual responsibility now for those who do preach and labour with doctrine, to approach this ministry and task with a double sense of responsibility to rightfully divide the Word of Truth.

Would you allow honour to frame your life and filter every expression?

Man was made a little lower than Elohim. What this implies is that God bestowed honour upon humanity. There are various spheres of authority within human government, the church, and the home. We are to give and to receive honour within these various spheres of authority according to scripture.

Honour in a believer's life is required to be a primary value system that is intentional and directed to the various spheres of authority. Christians are required to show honour to those whom honour is due.

WHAT IS DISHONOUR?

Dishonour is the lack or loss of honour or reputation. This implies the state of those who have lost honour or prestige, and this has resulted in shame being brought upon families. This shame can be seen as a cause of disgrace. Another definition of dishonour is to bring reproach or shame upon someone or something. It also implies that they will be treated with indignity and ultimately be unworthy in the sight of others. This stain of dishonour on the character of a person will lessen the reputation of a person who is to be trusted as they may appear to be someone who broke trust. Some of the character traits of dishonour in its purest form is to refuse, or to decline to accept responsibility to pay a bill, check, note, or draft which is due or presented.

Dishonour and its prevailing characteristics include:

- The state of being out of favour, the loss of favour, not being regarded, or respected.

- The conditions that follow being dishonoured are always covered with shame

- The cause of shame or a reproach as a result of dishonour always bring great discredit to a rational being who has succumbed to their vices.

- Being spiteful towards people and showing a great deal of unkindness.

- To be dismissive with no regard or respect.

- To devalue an individual by lowering their value.
- To treat one with disdain and disrespect

Greek words used for dishonour according to Strong's Concordance include:

Atimia pronounced as (at-ee-mee'-ah) and **Atimazo** pronounced as (at-im-ad'-zo) which mean 'in disgrace'.

Aischuno pronounced as (ahee-skhoo'-nom-ahee) which means 'I am ashamed and I am put to shame.'

Atimoo pronounced as (at-ee-mo'-o) which means 'to be treated shamefully'.

Epaischunomai means 'to be ashamed of and humiliated.'

Exaporeo – means 'to be utterly at a loss, to be in despair and completely disoriented'

Hebrew words used for dishonour according to Strong's concordance are:

Kelimmah which means 'insult, reproach, ignominy, disgrace, humiliation'

Kalam which means 'to be humiliated, ashamed, confounded and disgraced'

We can clearly see that both Greek and Hebrew words for dishonour identify very similar sobering warnings assigned to dishonour.

Understanding the power of honour and the curse of dishonour

Noah in his generation was considered righteous. He was

a man that was chosen by God because of his unwavering faith in God and the honour held in his heart follow the instructions of God. This was a time when a showdown was to be seen in the earth, yet Noah alone found favour with the Lord. Consider this man Noah and what he experienced. Fully awakened to the reality that his world as he knew it, was to end, Noah obeyed God's instruction and preached repentance for what seemed like an ever-increasing time – unwavering despite public ridicule. Interesting to point out is that we don't hear of any converts to this preaching. One could only imagine the terrible heartache, shame, confusion, utter regret and loss of the families who dishonoured him and the instructions he gave to them.

We know the story. Noah obeyed and his family were saved in the ark with all the animals. They finally left the ark and began to repopulate the earth. Now we cannot be certain to the exact reasons Noah found himself in a place of drunkenness. Maybe it was a result of survivor's guilt that so many were lost, and no one listened to him. Maybe he couldn't ascertain why God's will for salvation didn't include more people. Maybe he didn't feel worthy. Maybe the weight of the assignment overwhelmed him.

"And Noah began to be a farmer, and he planted a vineyard. Then he drank of the wine and was drunk, and became uncovered in his tent." Genesis 9:20-21

Let's look at the meaning of the words 'become uncovered'. The Hebrew word for this is "galah tavek". It describes to us how one removes himself from among his tent. Noah was not naked in his tent. It is widely believed that Noah separated himself as the watchman/guardian of his tent.

In other words, Noah absconded from his duties at home and his newfound love opened a door for this to be exploited. Noah's new love and hobby became a priority to him over and above his wife and family. This love drove Noah to spend more time in the vineyard than at home. We are faced with the same crisis today among the husbands and fathers. They love to be at work and when they're home, they're engaged with everything else but the family. This too can be seen as a separation of themselves from their tents.

> *"And Ham, the father of Canaan, saw the nakedness of his father, and told his two brothers outside."* Genesis 9:22

This story highlights who Ham is and the deep level of dishonour associated with his life, because Ham is the father of Canaan. The question that begs to be asked is why Canaan (Ham's son) is mentioned in the account of Ham seeing the nakedness of his father (this can also be linked to the nakedness of his mother). I can hear you asking, how? This is because Canaan was the illegitimate son of Noah's wife and his son Ham. Yes, you have heard correctly. Noah's wife and Noah's son had a child together. This account is recorded as a summary, because the detail of it is too shameful. The two brothers outside the tent is not an indication that they were accomplices to Ham's inappropriate behaviour. However, the word "outside" is the Hebrew word "chuwts" and is a root word which means 'to sever" or "separated by a wall." Shem and Japheth would not dare entering Noah's tent, except in extreme conditions of life and death, and honour or shame. In this case, the two of them entered Noah's tent backwards to cover their father's nakedness (and their mother's nakedness) with a garment, after Ham told them what happened. They did this to restore the dignity of their father and the family name. Noah would have had no other valid reason to curse Canaan to be a servant of servants to his brothers. Although Canaan would effectively be a brother to Shem and Japheth since he came from the same womb, the father's curse relegated him to a servant with no inheritance other than the benevolence of those whom he served.

We have an issue with absentee fathers, sometimes because they are emotionally unavailable, or they make work outside the city and come home once a term, or they may have simply deserted their responsibilities. We need the hearts of the fathers to be turned back to the son and the sons to their fathers. When fathers do not get involved in family matters, it leaves wives and mothers and children uncovered and unprotected. We cannot give the enemy any legroom.

Let's consider a historical account related to the British. From the British cultural inception, the British have been aggressive, bold, and often time defiant people. The British founding fathers were subjected to the rule and domination of kings and bishops, which created an unhealthy desire for freedom, which drove them to defiance. This defiance taught the British founding fathers to become lawless and reject state authority. The breakdown of family and society we are experiencing at large is down to the inherited behaviours of generations past not adhering the call of honour that helped shape so many cultures of the world successfully and peacefully.

It is plain to see that the preferences and desires of men wanting to be free of consequence and law drove them to abandon the foundation of culture called honour. Man's desire to be free imposed lawlessness above the restraints of the word of God in government, politics and economies. This thought was promoted to go unchallenged.

Despite the different histories of our nations, there is still an instruction to honour our leaders, the decision makers, our prime ministers and presidents. It has been very disturbing over the past decade to see, read and listen to how nations talk to and talk about their leaders. Even if you disagree, there is no greenlight from God to be outright demeaning and disrespectful. If you cannot respect those in authority and demonstrate that quality to your children, be careful that one day you are not the one eating the comments and disrespect from your children towards yourself – the same dishonour sown in days past.

> *"For rulers hold no terror for those who do right, but for those who do wrong. Do you want to be free from fear of the one in authority? Then do what is right and you will be commended. For the one in authority is God's servant for your good. But if you do wrong, be afraid, for rulers do not bear the sword for no reason. They are God's servants, agents of wrath to bring punishment on the wrongdoer. Therefore, it is necessary to submit to the authorities, not only because of possible punishment but also as a matter of conscience."* Romans 13:1-5 NIV

Be honourable in your giving, because blessing follows honour. Dishonour brings shame and limitation even financially. Let's explore the scriptures.

> *"Pay your obligations* to everyone: *taxes* to those
> *you* owe *taxes, tolls to those you* owe tolls, *respect* to
> those *you* owe *respect, and honour* to those *you* owe
> *honour."* Romans 13:7 CSB

God has mandated the authorities that exist in power over
us. Jesus even demonstrated removing a coin from the
mouth of the fish and instructing his disciples to give to
Caesar what was due. There is no license in the word of God
to dodge your financial responsibilities. We are actually encouraged to be more honourable, more faithful and more
truthful about financial matters and giving.

> *"Let as many bondservants as are under the yoke
> count their own masters worthy of all honour, so
> that the name of God and His doctrine may not be
> blasphemed."*1 Timothy 6:1 NKJV

Dishonour from servants or those serving is damaging to
the character of those in leadership. We are encouraged
here, that whatever team we serve and in whatever capacity
we hold under leadership, to give honour to our leaders
otherwise we clearly bring disrepute to ourselves by disre-
specting our leaders. I will explore this later, but honour
brings blessing and this then means that any dishonour
brings a curse and even a financial block to one's life and
one's organisation.

Ignoring widows brings dishonour

> *"Honour widows who are really widows."* 1 Timothy
> 5:3 NKJV

How often is this overlooked in our churches? We leave this instruction up to the old lady's intercessory group or the care ministry. This is pure religion. Honour the true widows.

> *"To him who sits on the throne and to the Lamb be blessing and HONOUR and glory and might forever and ever!"* Revelations 5:13 NKJV

The trap of distortion

One of the aims of the enemy is to bring people out of alignment with honour and cause their lives to dissolve into the dishonour arena. This does not mean someone starts out with an impure intention. I would like to share this story with you about those who started out with the best of intentions and then share the end result. Yes, I know it is always easier to see patterns, cycles and trends from the perspective of hindsight, but this is why continual evaluation of oneself and one's heart is so important.

The early American Christians who were Protestant had a fierce pioneering nature. They had observed the errors of Catholicism and began to address these. The manner in which they did this however became problematic. They persecuted and protested against everything that did not sound like them. They even at times protested against themselves.

For the ordinary person of that day, this was considered heroic and patriotic in their quest to protest. For the religious individual, it was considered courageous and noble to protest against a king and a pope. (How you may ask? Whenever prophets in the Old Testament came to address the captivity of Israel by foreign kings such as Assyrian and Babylonian kings, their position was one of defiance against those kings).

This position of extreme protest in order to bring about change in America has left a pattern of confrontational spirituality that has become part of the mainstream culture and communication strategy for both religious and non-religious alike. Culture is not always obvious. The subtle culture of being grated at the idea of honouring those in leadership is a real point of consideration.

If we are truly honest, there is something inside of us that makes it difficult for the average Westerner (and I say Westerner here as honour operates differently in other cultures) to embrace the idea and mandate that everyone should be honoured, even those who hold different viewpoints to oneself. Many years later, we see the effects of the great divides within American politics and the dishonour that is continually thrown at each opposing side by leaders and constituents alike. There are no perfect leaders, but we are instructed to both honour and pray for our leaders. Our feelings cannot trump the principle of the Word of God.

Food for thought

Q: Do you complain about your boss or manager?

Q: Do you badmouth the spiritual leaders in your life?

Q: Do you talk about the pastors critically in front of your children?

Q: Do you find yourself angry at leadership and the leadership structure?

Q: Do you find it difficult to compliment other's success?

THE TWIN TOWERS

The purpose of a pillar is to support the structure of a building. The pillars of honour are supported and intertwined in the characteristics of loyalty and faithfulness. These two characteristics support and underpin a believer's life to build a life of honour. May faithfulness and loyalty be an ever-present feature to your life of honour? In the same manner that Aaron and Hur held up the hands of Moses, so loyalty and faithfulness underpins the instruction to walk in honour. To live the live of honour we are talking about requires us to explore loyalty and faithfulness in greater depth.

Loyalty is:

- The act of binding yourself
- Faithfulness and commitment
- Devotion and allegiance
- Reliability

Loyalty is what you do, not just what you say. Loyalty operates in your heart. It is willing and not reluctant; unwavering in allegiance. For instance, being faithful in allegiance to one's lawful sovereign or government i.e. being loyal to the king.

When you study the historical account of Edom aka Esau, who we know sold his birth right, he was disloyal to the requirements of firstborn inheritance. He did not place value on what God had ordered. As a result, he lost more than just his birth right and this had a generational impact on his bloodline. Disloyalty has consequences.

"I will bring you plummeting down," said the Lord. (Obadiah 1:4-14, especially verses 4 and 11)

Let's consider a biblical account for loyalty.

"A friend loves at all times, and a brother is born for adversity" Proverbs 17:17 NKJV

According to 1 Samuel 18, it is widely known amongst scholars that the heart of Jonathan was knitted to the heart of David. It is recorded that Jonathan made a covenant with David because their brotherly love for each other ran deep. This covenant remained intact even when Saul, Jonathan's dad and King, wanted to kill David. Yet Jonathan still loved David and still honoured their covenant. Even at the place of Jonathan's death, because of the covenant of Jonathan and David, David showed kindness to Mephibosheth. This was because he was a son of Saul and Jonathan's house. Jonathan's loyalty to David was not fake or forced. True loyalty must come from an authentic relationship with God and with others.

The lessons of loyalty are:

- Loyalty does not waver
- Loyalty is not always easy and cheap
- Loyalty is more than lip service
- Loyalty and honour underpin God-relationships
- Loyalty is not exempt because of extenuating circumstances

- Loyalty must be backed by action; the same applies to honour

---

The very ministry of Jesus was an extension of His loyalty and faithfulness to the vision of Father God for all of humanity.

Jesus did not honour God with verbal assurances only, but did what was required, obeyed and sacrificed even unto death so that God's will could prevail.

"Be not deceived, God is not mocked whatsoever a man sows that shall he reap" Galatians 6:7 NKJV

If we are involved in sowing disloyalty or seeds of disloyalty, then one can count on the fact that what we sow soon becomes what we reap. What you speak becomes what you eat. If you don't want dishonour to be your portion, stop sowing dishonour to others. This requires more than just restraint. True honour can only come from a life that has allowed and continues to allow Father God to process. My friend, make up your mind and determine in your heart that your life will have no landing pads for helicopters carrying dishonour. Determine that your life of Christianity will be underpinned, covered and intertwined in your fabric with honour, honour and more honour.

Loyalty requires sacrifice and will have demands. Your loyalty will be tested at some point. You can count on that. Opportunity to be offended will come; challenging scenarios that are uncomfortable and test the loyalty will come. We have to choose to have a good relationship with truth. If we don't, disloyalty becomes a real threat. I would go as far to say that one couldn't trust a relationship where sacrifice has not supported the verbal assurance of loyalty and honour.

Our life decisions made will follow our list of priorities or one can call it allegiance list.

Consider your life, your time, your giving, your perspectives. They will tell you who your allegiance is to. Real questions will allow us to have real answers. Transformation occurs at a place of truth. When we can start to be truthful with ourselves, God can begin to remove what is not of Him, what is not authentic, what is not good for our lives and prophetic destinies.

Food for thought

Q: Is your allegiance to God?

Q: Is your allegiance to your spiritual family?

Q: Is your allegiance to the purpose of advancement for the Kingdom of God?

Q: Is your allegiance to your biological family?

Q: Is your allegiance to money?

Q: Is your allegiance to your friends?

"And Naomi said to her two daughters-in-law, 'Go, each return to her mother's house. The Lord deal kindly with you, as you have dealt with the dead and with me.' Then Naomi said to her daughter-in-law, 'blessed be he of the Lord, who has not forsaken His kindness to the living and the dead. The man is a relative of ours, a near kinsman.' Then he said, 'Blessed are you of the Lord, my daughter! For you have shown more kindness at the end than at the beginning, in that you did not go after young men, whether poor or rich" Ruth 1:8*

There is a type of love Ruth had for Naomi. If we look at this word in the Old Testament, it is **'Hesed'**, which means loyal love. It is not a feeling or mood type of love. It is a love that requires action and sacrifice to support it regardless of one's own feelings on the matter. It is not a matter of what is convenient or easy, or fast. Hesed is also translated as a kindness.

In the story of Ruth and Naomi, Boaz mentions that she could have had a young man to remarry but her loyal love meant that the only consideration was whatever helped Naomi.

Lastly, loyalty to God will always be rewarded. Do not believe the lie of the enemy that it is not worth it. God is not a man that He would lie. He will honour His promises to you. Do not give up on the qualities of honour, loyalty and faithfulness, because our God 'HE IS FAITHFUL and TRUE' and will reward each and every one of you.

According to the Merriam-Webster Dictionary, the definition of faithfulness is:

- steadfast in affection or allegiance
- firm in adherence to promises or in observance of duty
- given with strong assurance
- true to the facts, to a standard, or to an original

Faithfulness is:

- Consistency and reliability
- Steadfast and staunch
- Being resolute in one's decisions and purposes
- Having others being able to lean and depend on you

Faithfulness can be expressed in relation to a cause, ideal, custom, institution, or faithfulness to a product. Being faithful will imply a person does not stray from an oath or promise made and that their word and behaviour can be trusted i.e. they do not change allegiances often or easily.

Let's explore biblical accounts of faithfulness.

Psalm 25:10 in the New King James Version says *'All the paths of the* LORD *are mercy and truth, To such as keep His covenant and His testimonies.'*

The most well-known and persistent example of God's faithfulness to mankind would be the difficult relationship between the people of the Kingdom of Israel and God himself. Israel, if you consider the many years documented in the Old Testament were extremely unfaithful.

Despite their blatant unfaithfulness, God is quite demonstrative about His love and bond to them. He instructs his prophet to marry a prostitute to demonstrate that he is bonded to them, betrothed to them and committed to the covenant established with them because HE is faithful even when we are not.

"I will betroth you to Me in faithfulness, And you shall know the LORD." Hosea 2:20 NKJV

Consider this. Can you imagine being asked by God to marry a prostitute? I mean you, a faithful, honourable, holy man of God, and this is what your Heavenly Father requests of you in order to fulfil His plan. How loyal must Prophet Hosea have been to honour that request and sacrifice required by heaven.

As followers of God, we need to demonstrate the same qualities of faithfulness, love, kindness, loyalty and commitment that our Father exhibits.

"Moreover it is required in stewards that one be found faithful" 1 Corinthians 4:2 NKJV

"If we are faithless, He remains faithful; He cannot deny Himself." 2 Timothy 2:13 NKJV

Epaphrus and Tychicus are identified as faithful ministers of Christ in Colossians 1:7 ; 4:7.

"And I thank Christ Jesus our Lord who has enabled me, because He counted me faithful, putting me into the ministry" 1 Timothy 1:12 NKJV

I pose this one question to you …

Q: Can God call you and I faithful?

THE ENEMIES OF HONOUR

The enemies of honour are:

- Jezebel spirit
- Absalom spirit
- Korah spirit
- Adonija spirit
- Leviathan spirit

The War to Undermine Honour

The intention of the local Church is to expand the Kingdom of God throughout the globe. There has always been constant warfare in the bid to advance the agenda of heaven and warfare against just that. Throughout every generation these attacks may vary. We however, have seen a consistent and steady decline in humanity against operating in the principles of honour, and this philosophy has crept into the Church and held leaders captive and fearful to express their concern regarding the lack of honour and the apparent and clear rebellion in the hearts of people.

Enemies of Honour:

The Jezebel Spirit

"Nevertheless I have a few things against you, because you allow that woman Jezebel, who calls herself a prophetess, to teach and seduce My servants to com-

> *mit sexual immorality and eat things sacrificed to
> idols"* Revelation 2:20 NKJV

The Jezebel spirit is not a physical woman or a person; it is a spirit that influences the person. A jezebel spirit is a leadership strategy of the enemy that targets weak leadership. Jezebel attacks the weakest link in the structure and attaches itself to the weak link and maneuvers like a snake meandering its way to the head of an organization. It controls leaders from behind the scenes and lives its fantasies through leadership. Jezebel is always associated with drunkenness, which implies that it numbs and dominates your ability to be sober and coherent in your thoughts and decision-making.

The spirit of Jezebel seeks to attain information about leadership to influence their decisions through domination and control to benefit this spirit. Another tactic of Jezebel is to entice fear in leadership thus resulting in leaders absconding from their assignments. Jezebel initiates slander against God-appointed leadership. Churches affected by the spirit of jezebel will be misaligned to inaccurate doctrine. This misalignment will affect the lifestyle of believers if a spirit of jezebel is entertained. There is only one way of dealing with Jezebel and that's through prayer and head on confrontation.

> *'The jezebel spirit is like a black widow spider, which
> is deadly and will even eat its own mate'.* John Paul
> Jackson, Unmasking the Jezebel Spirit in 2002.

The Absalom Spirit

> "And Absalom rose up early, and stood beside the way of the gate: and it was so, that when any man that had a controversy and came to the king for judgment, then Absalom called unto him, and said, Of what city art thou? And he said, Thy servant is of one of the tribes of Israel. And on this manner did Absalom to all Israel that came to the king for judgment: **so Absalom stole the hearts of the men of Israel**. And Absalom sent for Ahithophel the Gilonite, David's counsellor, from his city, even from Giloh, while he offered sacrifices. And the conspiracy was strong; for the people increased continually with Absalom." 2 Samuel 15:2,6,12 NKJV

Absalom embodied sedition in his life by rebelling against his father King David and tried to take the kingdom from King David. Absalom was full of pride, vanity and arrogance and saw himself as an equal to King David and coveted what was not allotted to him.

Betrayal and treachery always follow an Absalom spirit. Leaders ought to watch against this divisive spirit that seeks to separate and break up churches. Absalom initiated and incited the people to rebel against the God-given authority of David who was the rightful king. Absalom seduced people to side with his agenda against King David.

'An Absalom spirit will manipulate many people to gain their trust to shift them onto their side, against leadership. This spirit is deceptive and cunning in how it lures people to its agenda. This spirit works its rebellion in the shadows. This spirit embodies an unbridled ambition, which is very subtle and crafty in its attempt to go after the Father figure or leader. The Absalom spirit is likened to a snake sliding between the people to attack the leader. One of the roles of prophetic ministry is to shammar. To shammar means to "to see" hidden conspiracies and expose them before it's too late. Shammar also means "to protect.'"

The Adonijah spirit

> *"Then Adonijah the son of Haggith exalted himself, saying, "I will be king"; and he prepared for himself chariots and horsemen, and fifty men to run before him. (And his father had not rebuked him at any time by saying, "Why have you done so?" He was* also very good-looking. *His mother* had borne him after Absalom.) Then he conferred with Joab the son of *Zeruiah and with Abiathar the priest, and they followed and helped Adonijah. But Zadok the priest, Benaiah the son of Jehoiada, Nathan the prophet, Shimei, Rei, and the mighty men who belonged* to David were not with Adonijah." 1 Kings 1:5-10 NKJV

Adonijah represents a renegade spirit that deploys seduction and pretense to achieve its wickedness. The spirit of Adonijah always uses seduction to undermine and destroy the purposes of God and the potential of people by having influence and authority over all men and women of God (those that stand in leadership).

The spirit of adonijah identifies with people who share common issues that harbor bitterness and unforgiveness, and it seeks to gain control by an old war tactic of divide and conquer. This spirit always seeks to transfer loyalty from one person to another. This spirit defies divine authority by using cunningness and craftiness in its conspiracy to usurp God given authority. It forms wicked alliances that breed treason, deception and vanity.

5 Characteristics of the Adonijah Spirit

1. Self-Promotion – Pride always motivates a deviation from the intention of God. Pride is a manifestation from the root of bitterness.

2. 'I will' - This heart is postured against the will of God. The Throne wasn't his to take but Solomon's inheritance. The root of this is rejection.

3. Chariots - This deals with doctrine. This spirit attacks the doctrine of a leader. It typified his heart and evil desire to raise his own doctrine and this gave this error mobility.

4. Horsemen -These are riders of chariots. They drove and fortified Adonijah's position of betrayal.

5. 50 men - 50 deals with jubilee and freedom, and 'men' represents flesh. The order of God was violated here because it was always the prophets that blew the horn announcing jubilee and freedom. Here we see the arm of flesh announcing and marketing the supposedly new-found and ill-gained freedom.

Scripture tells us that those who belonged to David were NOT with Adonijah. Make sure that this spirit knows where you belong because YOUR SILENCE will bring death. Honour will always be tested. The key to overcoming the seduction of this spirit is the spirit of loyalty, the heart of a servant that exemplifies humility. Benaiah still remained loyal, trustworthy, a man of integrity and did not defect. It was made clear that Benaiah was not in agreement with the treason that was unfolding. You cannot remain silent when such a spirit is seeking to overthrow God's appointed leadership.

The Korah Spirit

> *"Now Korah, the son of Izhar, the son of Kohath, the son of Levi, and Dathan and Abiram, the sons of Eliab, and On, the son of Peleth, sons of Reuben, took men: 2 And they rose up before Moses, with certain of the children of Israel, two hundred and fifty princes of the assembly, famous in the congregation, men of renown: 3 And they gathered themselves together against Moses and against Aaron, and said unto them, Ye take too much upon you, seeing all the congregation are holy, every one of them, and the LORD is among them: wherefore then lift ye up yourselves above the congregation of the LORD?"* Numbers 16:1-3 NKJV

Korah's rebellion was more defiant than Absalom. Korah made his rebellion against the leadership of Moses and Aaron publically known. Korah believed that Moses exalted himself above other leaders. Korah led many to believe that Moses was holding the other leaders down. It is widely believed that a Jezebel spirit appears to work primarily through women, but here the Korah spirit operates primarily through men. I personally don't believe these spirits are limited to operate in this way only. As we know, 'rebellion is as the sin of witchcraft.' To combat a spirit of revolt in a church it's imperative that Prophets are seen to stand and support leadership to ensure that destruction is not brought to that church.

The Leviathan Spirit

"In that day the LORD with His severe sword, great and strong, Will punish Leviathan the fleeing serpent,Leviathan that twisted serpent; And He will slay the reptile that is in the sea." Isaiah 27:1 NKJV

Leviathan is the king over all children of pride. The crocodile is a representation of a Leviathan spirit which attacks Godly leaders with pride causing them to become arrogant and puffed up. This spirit drives leaders to deviate from the original plan of God, which ultimately says to God I know better than you.

"God resists the proud and gives grace to the humble." 1 Peter 5:5 NKJV

The characteristics of the spirit of Leviathan are:

- lack of prayer
- mean spirited
- disregard to covenant
- no servanthood in their lives
- not awakened to the move of the spirit of God
- lack of adaptability
- stiff necked and hardness of heart
- pride

Pride opens doors for destruction.

"Pride goeth before destruction, and an haughty spirit before a fall." Proverbs 16:18 NKJV

The protection of a church is lost if the gates are destroyed. Gates are entry points into that community and culture of believers. Strongholds are established if these spirits are able to enter into that community. The gate is a place of authority, and the enemy always attacks the gate to unseat that authority so that he can wreak havoc in that community. This is why watchmen and women of God are so vital. The altars and walls need to be manned 24/7. The people within that community cannot advance against the enemy's tactics unless they are in submission to someone who has credible authority to do so. The gate is a place where the enemy is challenged and rebuked. To rebuke means to force back. A rebuke is a sharp reprimand. A reprimand is a severe or formal rebuke by a person in authority.

To walk in a place of total honour, one has to be conscious and aware of the words that come out of their mouths alongside the corresponding behaviours that support the posture of our hearts and words. Victory in the area of honour is first and foremost a decision that needs to be made to be free from the control of the opinions of man, yet secure in the promises of God's word. This means a conscious decision needs to be made regarding what we allow into our gates and what we don't allow. This will ultimately determine our freedom or our entrapment. In the absence of honour, we become the playground for seducing spirits to shift us out of a place of stability into the cauldrons of oppression that leads to possession. Remember, rebellion disarms the stable and stimulates dysfunction.

A FEW GOOD MEN

David's Mighty Men

There are few men in the Bible that attract our attention as much as David. He is mentioned more than any other man in the Bible except Jesus. His choices regarding his mighty men are to be examined. He is the only man in the Word of God who is called "a man after God's own heart."

The Bible tells us as Christians that the things written in the Old Testament were written for our example. I believe that the journey to understanding the power of "The Honour Code" is to examine the life of David, because the men that surrounded David and who were considered to be his mighty men displayed loyalty, honour and sacrifice.

> "These are the names of the mighty men whom David had: Josheb-Basshebeth the Tachmonite, chief among the captains. He was called Adino the Eznite, because he had killed eight hundred men at one time. 2 Samuel 23:8 NKJV

The day of the one-man show is no longer relevant. This is not to say we do not believe God has an order and uses the set man or woman of the house. This points to an emphasis on team ministry and the power and importance of a Godly team. We can clearly see through the life of David and his mighty men how valuable a Godly team is. Why are they

considered the mighty men? These men were brave, courageous, mighty, loyal and anointed with power of God. They
did not shy away from sacrifice and lived fully in service
of the king. The standard of their service to King David is
a template for us. In this passage in 2 Samuel 23, we will
notice some "stories." David at the end of his life reflects
over his journey and recounts the mighty men of valour.

Let me introduce you to one of David's mighty men
whose name was Benaiah.

*"Now these were the heads of the mighty men whom
David had, who strengthened themselves with him
in his kingdom, with all Israel, to make him king,
according to the word of the Lord concerning Israel"*
1 Chronicles 11:10 NKJV

*"And this is the number of the mighty men whom Da-
vid had: Jashobeam the son of a Hachmonite, chief of
the captains; he had lifted up his spear against three
hundred, killed by him at one time. After him was
Eleazar the son of Dodo, the Ahohite, who was one
of the three mighty men. He was with David at Pas-
dammim. Now there the Philistines were gathered for
battle, and there was a piece of ground full of barley.
So the people fled from the Philistines. But they sta-
tioned themselves in the middle of that field, defend-
ed it, and killed the Philistines. So the Lord brought
about a great victory.* 1 Chronicles 11:10-14 NKJV

*"Abishai the brother of Joab was chief of another
three. He had lifted up his spear against three hundred men, killed them, and won a name among these*

three. Of the three he was more honoured than the other two men. Therefore he became their captain. However he did not attain to the first three. Benaiah was the son of Jehoiada, the son of a valiant man from Kabzeel, who had done many deeds. He had killed two lion-like heroes of Moab. He also had gone down and killed a lion in the midst of a pit on a snowy day. And he killed an Egyptian, a man of great height, five cubits tall. In the Egyptian's hand there was a spear like a weaver's beam; and he went down to him with a staff, wrested the spear out of the Egyptian's hand, and killed him with his own spear. These things Benaiah the son of Jehoiada did, and won a name among three mighty men. Indeed he was more honoured than the thirty, but he did not attain to the first three. And David appointed him over his guard. 1 Chronicles 11: 20-25 NKJV

Who was Benaiah? Benaiah was a fearless warrior and valiant fighter. He was known for the great exploits he performed.

- He was known for killing two of Moab's best warriors (2 lion-like men)

- He killed a lion in the midst of a pit on a snowy day.

- He killed an Egyptian, a man of great height, five cubits tall. (2.25 metres)

- He earned a name among the three infamous mighty men of David

- Out of David's thirty men, he was more honoured than any other

- David appointed him over his guard.

- In the Egyptian's hand there was a spear and he went down to him with a staff, wrestled the spear out of the Egyptian's hand, and killed him with his own spear.

> **The same grace that was upon David was upon Benaiah. He walked in oneness with his leader**

Adino

Adino was also a mighty man of valour. He had an encounter where he was massively outnumbered by eight hundred to one (we can read this account in 2 Samuel 23:8 NKJV).

My question is, how does one man with a spear fight off 800 men. What kind of man was he?

- He was a man who didn't give up when he was outnumbered.

- He was a man of loyalty and courage.

- He didn't turn and run away from his assignment.

- His courage and his strength came from God.

Eleazar

Eleazar was another mighty man of David's. He was known as the man with a sword (see 2 Samuel 23:9-10 NKJV). He was one with his sword, meaning to say he wielded his sword with precision and used it as a defence against the enemy. Today we have a sword - the word of God, given to us to wield against the enemy. Are we known as being one with our sword, the Word?

> *"For the word of God is quick, and powerful, and sharper than any two edged sword, piercing even to the dividing asunder of soul and spirit, and of the joints and marrow, and is a discerner of the thoughts and intents of the heart."* Hebrews 4:12 NKJV

> *"And take the helmet of salvation, and the sword of the Spirit, which is the word of God"* Ephesians 6:17 NKJV

Shammah

Shammah was an extremely brave warrior and part of David's mighty men.

> *"And after him was* Shammah *the son of Agee the Hararite. The Philistines had gathered together into a troop where there was a piece of ground full of lentils. So the people fled from the Philistines. But he stationed himself in the middle of the field, defended it, and killed the Philistines. So the* LORD *brought about a great victory."* 2 Samuel 23:11-12 NKJV

He stood when others fled. He knew his purpose, he understood the impact of his decision and he stood irrespective of the danger. This man of valour risked everything for a pea patch because it belonged to the King. When everyone else fled, he stood his ground and fought. We often allow our eyes to view what others are doing and get discouraged. Shammah didn't care if he was the only one that cared. He was going to do what was right.

Why did he fight? It was only a patch of beans. The King had his honour at stake and his enemy was coming for the pea patch whilst the people were hungry and required food. And Shammah stood his ground. Remember, they fought physical enemies in the Old Testament. We fight spiritual enemies today. The very important question to our hearts is, will we stand and fight for what belongs to the King? Are we prepared to stand-alone for what is right?

What else do we know of these Mighty Men? There was an occasion when King David was known to be thirsty and desired a drink of water from a brook that had sweet water. The challenge was that this brook was located in the enemy's territory. These mighty men of David risked going into the enemy's territory to retrieve water for King David.

Were they commanded by David to get the cup of water? NO. Were they compelled by duty to get the cup of water? NO. They went because they loved their King. Why were they so loyal?

There were three classes of these men who came to David in his rejection as King.

- There were those who came in distress because they were persecuted by Saul
- There were those who were in debt and about to be sold into slavery.
- There were those who were discontented and unhappy with what life had to offer. Life had not been good to them.

So as a result, we see an army, David's army, made up of many men with many reasons or agendas for being part of the army. The question to consider is what made the Mighty Men of Valour stand out from among the rest?

The amazing and mighty men of valour, the mighty men of David, loved their King. Their level of honour, sacrifice and loyalty is worthy of a double mention. Their commitment was first rate. They never wavered ever. You see, they came to him in different states of need and distress and David helped them. Their commitment to David extended throughout his tenure as both anointed and then finally crowned King of Israel and Judah. They were loyal and faithful and loved not their lives even unto death. We see through scripture Jesus stating that 'he who wants to gain his life must be prepared to lose it.' This is the characteristic that embodied David's mighty men.

My encouragement to you in this hour is to embrace the heart posture of honour, loyalty, and display this through your faithfulness to God and his appointed leaders.

Does our commitment to God and honour to the Father continue even when our status changes? It is easy to come to God in distress, when you are sick, when you are broke, when you are in despair. When God begins to elevate you and change your health, wealth, status and identity – are you one who will consider the agenda of heaven an inconvenience, or the call of God an obstacle? Will you be one who will honour your King until your dying day?

STAY THE PROCESS

"David therefore departed from there and escaped to the cave of Adullam. So when his brothers and his father's entire house heard it, they went down there to him. 2 And everyone who was in distress, everyone who was in debt, and everyone who was discontented gathered to him. So he became captain over them. And there were about four hundred men with him." 1 Samuel 22:1-2 NKJV

David inherited a kingdom from King Saul that had many problems. One of these major problems that David inherited was the absence of God's presence, symbolised by the ark of God. The ark of God also represents God honouring you with His presence because you were honourable in your ways.

The ark of God was captured by the Philistines in 1 Samuel 4, before Saul became king. The ark of God was lost under the priesthood and watch of Eli, the high priest. Since this moment, the glory of God had departed from Israel (1 Samuel 4:21) meaning that God's presence was not with Israel. The ark of God was eventually returned to Israel, because the Lord punished the Philistines, who had to return the ark of God back to the nation of Israel (1 Samuel 5-6). The Ark was returned to the people of Beth Shemesh. Unfortunately for them, they disobeyed protocols and looked into the ark. More than fifty thousand men were slain by the Lord for irreverence and dishonouring the sacred ordinances and instructions of God. The ark of God was then taken to Kirjath Jearim, to the house of Abinadad on the hill (1 Samuel 7:1). It remained here for a very long time (20 years). All the house of Israel lamented after the Lord. In the aftermath of this, the demand for a king arose (1 Samuel 8). This did not please the Lord. Saul was chosen as king in the absence of the Ark of the Covenant. When David becomes king over all Israel one of the first things he did was to bring back the ark of God and restore the honour of God back into Israel. He conquers the Philistines (who had first captured the Ark and who also defeated and killed Saul), 2 Samuel 5:17-25. It is then that David seeks to bring the ark back, but he does not do so according to the plan of the Lord. Uzzah touched the ark irreverently and dishonoured the pattern in how to move the ark of God, and the Lord killed him. The ark of God was left at the house of Obed-Edom, until David prepared to bring it back. David brought the ark of God back to the house of Judah and once it was returned, the place of honour was restored to the house of Judah. The Lord then made a covenant with David in that place.

Now I have shared much in order to show you this. The good intentions of our hearts are never a substitute or an excuse for circumventing the principles and processes of God. God is not a man and that means he cannot lie. If He has given instructions or commands and agreed the consequences, then He cannot go back on his own word because He is bound to His Word.

We see a pattern of occasions where others have considered their actions justifiable, but the consequence unfortunately was death. Now we do not live in the Old Testament or live under the law but in the same way, we still have to embrace the protocols, principles and patterns of Gods Word for our lives. It is a dangerous thing to assume we know better or that we can access what He has promised without submitting fully to God.

The following scripture is very sobering.

"because, although they knew God, they did not glorify Him as God, nor were thankful, but became futile in their thoughts, and their foolish hearts were darkened." Romans 1:21 NKJV

When we persist in going in our own direction or living life by our own wisdom, as believers we can end up in a difficult place in our walk with God. The purpose of this book and the understanding I desire to bring to your heart is that we have a loving and mighty Father and He desires the best for us. We must however be willing to be all in. We cannot choose the elements of kingdom living we prefer and expect the outcomes to match. It's a matter of total love, total surrender and total obedience.

> **David's mighty men were able to walk in unprecedented levels of power, breakthrough and victory as we shared earlier in the chapter. I believe this was possible because of their heart posture and life of complete surrender to their King. They had endorsement from heaven.**

THE BENEFITS OF HONOUR

The benefits of honour are as follows:

- Long life
- Promotion
- Increase
- Reversing the curse
- Blessing
- Prosperity and favour

Long life

> *"Children, obey your parents in the Lord, for this is right. "Honour your father and mother," which is the first commandment with promise: "that it may be well with you and you may live long on the earth." And you, fathers, do not provoke your children to wrath, but bring them up in the training and admonition of the Lord."* Ephesians 6:1-4 NKJV

In these verses, the apostle Paul aims to encourage us that despite the various temptations and subtle invitations of dishonour, we are to be steadfast in how we conduct ourselves to those in authority over us, most notably our parents. No matter how intense the warfare may get to sway us away from our founding value of honour, it is a prerequisite to remain honourable, and in turn this posture of heart and behavioural attitude will preserve your life from the realm of premature death. There are a considerable amount of benefits associated with honour. It would be worthy to mention here that the instruction to honour does not come with conditions. For example, do you honour your parents only when you are in agreement with the way in which they lead the family? No. Do you only honour your parents when you like how they are treating you and speaking to you? No. Do you only honour your parents because they 'nice' people? No. Our mandate to honour our parents goes beyond our opinions and interests. When we obey fully, we also fully receive the promise in His Word for us.

Promotion

Promotion from God is never lateral. Promotion from God always takes you higher than where you were previously. The way to access this promotion from God is to be a faithful steward of God-given assignment because to be faithful over a little is to be faithful over much. Desire to be found to be a servant of all, to walk in humility, because these character traits underpin the pathway to promotion from God.

In God's wisdom, the way up is down. Advancement up the career ladder is a universal and consuming drive. The reasons are usually more money, more prestige, and more power. We can ascertain that in the Kingdom of God the way up is down.

> *"Humble yourselves under the mighty hand of God, that He may exalt you in due time"* 1 Peter 5:6 NKJV

The account of David's life typifies a life of submission and honour, which ultimately brought promotion to him. There were struggles and setbacks for sure. There were also lots of opportunities for promotion that didn't always come packaged as a promotion. David navigated these encounters with honour.

When the prophet was looking for the next King, David was located shepherding. After being anointed king, but not yet serving as crowned King, David became a minstrel in the courts of the palace. Even throughout the new appointment given to him by King Saul, he was sober and measured in his new tasks. This was all a test of his character because God's promotion was about to come into his life. David knew God would exalt him at the right time in His own way. Years later when Saul was trying to kill David and David found himself in the position to take Saul out, David chose honour. He did not manipulate the circumstances based on prophetic anointing that took place years earlier. In this moment David decided to humble himself under the hand of God instead of choosing to lay a hand on Saul, and this revealed his level of honour. The level of honour and submission David walked in is highlighted even more at Saul's death. David hesitated to assume the throne. The men of Judah had to come to David to anoint him king of Judah. Then it was seven years before the remainder of the tribes requested David's rule.

Continue to be diligent in your stewardship of your responsibilities. Humble yourself under the mighty hand of God because in due time He will promote you. Don't rush this process.

Reversing the curse

*"And Jabez was **more honourable** than his brethren*

> *And Jabez called on the God of Israel, saying, Oh that*
> *thou wouldest bless me indeed, and enlarge my coast,*
> *and that thine hand might be with me, and that thou*
> *wouldest keep [me] from evil, that it may not grieve*
> *me! And God granted him that which he requested."*
> 1 Chronicles 4:9-10 NKJV

Now Jabez was named by his mother at his birth when she was in extreme pain. Every time his named is called out, it is a reminder of the sorrow he brought her at birth. But the Bible states that he was more honourable than his brothers. There are scholars who believe this text should actually read 'more honoured' than his brothers. Now either way, I think it is saying the same thing. Honour is ours to give. So if he was more honoured, then those around him considered him worthy to give their honour to. And if we use the first version, he was more honourable in his actions. Either way, honour formed the fabric of Jabez's life despite his starting point. Here we see a very short story in scripture where Jabez cried out to God in prayer and made a request for increase, enlargement and protection. God heard and granted his request. Jabez's story was changed. Centuries later, here we are all praying the prayer of Jabez for the Lord to enlarge our tents. How significant is that? Honour can rewrite your story. How many of you are with me on this one? Maybe our background or status or starting points have not been ideal BUT we have a GOD who is awesome, who is listening, who is more than able to CHANGE OUR STORY.

Blessing

Honour has the ability to unlock both blessings and generational blessing over your life, and this implies divine favour, prosperity and happiness. Blessing in the bible is mentioned three times more than cursing. Blessing is a pronunciation over our lives, which imparts spiritual power, assurance, approval, confidence and a grace that allows us to be and walk in what God desires for us. The greatest pronunciation of blessing comes from the Father.

Almost every blessing in the Bible is of a generational nature. Generational blessing is a blessing that can be passed onto the next generation. In essence, a blessing which a father or mother can pass onto their children and their children's children. According to Strong's Complete Concordance of the Bible, one Hebrew word for prosperity is 'shalom'. We often associate the word shalom with peace, but it is also "completeness, soundness, welfare and peace." A kind of peace and blessing where there is nothing missing, nothing broken, and you are made complete or whole. The purpose of blessing is to make you whole. To bring a complete and mature picture of Christ to your life that is sealed in the peace of God.

Let's look at the account of Jacob and Esau. Esau despised what God loved. Esau was also deceitful in his nature, which many do not focus on. Esau did not value his birth right or his inheritance, and in a moment of hunger and weakness he lost his birth right to his younger brother Jacob. Esau lost his blessing. The pronunciation of blessing was declared over Jacob. We cannot receive blessing and inheritance from those we despise. We cannot only honour and value the great men of God gone by such as John Wesley, Smith Wigglesworth and William Seymour to name a few, yet carry disdain in our hearts for our local leaders and pastors who preach and carry us week in and week out. How can you receive a pronunciation of blessing into a well that carries dishonour? It is fair to say that blessing and honour go hand in hand.

I have seen during my time in ministry, how those who carry dishonour push away the very breakthrough and blessing they desire because dishonour and blessing are like oil and water. They do not mix.

Prosperity and favour

When you begin to walk in the favour and blessing of the Lord, others will recognize it. The favour and blessing of God on your life is one of the most powerful things you can have.

Joseph experienced God's favour from a very young age and his favour became problematic. He was bestowed a gift from his father, and it caused him to be despised by his brothers. He had prophetic dreams, which they also despised because of the interpretation. They sold him into slavery and this set Joseph on a journey that took him to Potiphar's house. Potiphar's wife tried to seduce him and Joseph chose the more honourable way and he fled.

He ended up in prison and operated honourably even in lockup. He was promoted in prison. When you walk in honour, promotion will find you wherever you are. His spirit of excellence and attitude of honour caused him to be promoted by God to the second highest position in Egypt where Joseph was able to provide strategy to a nation that became a lifeline during the famine.

Your decision to walk in honour, will cause your circumstances to have to change. Your decision to honour

God, honour your leaders and honour others around you will force circumstances to eventually line up to your prophetic destiny. Don't succumb to pressures to engage in dishonourable conversations or acts. Choose honour and let honour choose you for breakthroughs beyond your expectations. When you have God's favour and blessing, there is nothing in life that can hold you down.

Matthew 6:33 says, *"Seek first the kingdom of God and His righteousness, and all these things shall be added to you"*

A More Excellent Way

This entire book has been an encouragement to walk in the way of honour.

When we look at the Godhead, God the Father, Jesus the Son and the person of the Holy Spirit, we see a beautiful picture of honour – more than once in scripture.

- When Jesus was baptised in the river, the heavens opened, and God publicly honoured his son Jesus and affirmed him. That pronunciation is also a Fatherly blessing over the life of Jesus (Matthew 3:13-17)

- I've shared earlier how honour requires one to act on the instruction of the one in authority. At the very beginning of creation, God spoke, and the Holy spirit honoured his command and acted on the Words of God (Genesis 1:2)

- Another picture of honour would be when Jesus was at the garden of Gethsemane and God had required Jesus to obey unto death. Jesus prayed for this cup to pass but Jesus ultimately obeyed His Father's instructions and trusted the process God had in mind for our salvation (Mark 14:32-50)

Other examples of honour in the life of Jesus are:

- Jesus humbling himself and allowing God to exalt Him in due time

- Jesus followed his father's will and didn't seek his own (the test in the wilderness)

- Jesus provided the definition for greatness - being servant of all to be great in the kingdom

- Before Jesus commenced ministry, at a wedding his mother asked him to perform a miracle. He felt it wasn't time, but honoured his mother's request. Jesus was under submission.

One of Satan's most effective traps for believers, seems to be offense. This is a huge factor in so many people falling away from destiny, purpose and connection.

In marriage, you have the 80/20 rule. You don't get everything you want in a single person – in general you get about 80 percent. Marriage troubles come when a spouse leaves the 80 percent and goes hunting for the missing 20. In hindsight, they often begin to realise they end up with 20 but lost a massive 80. The same happens in church life. No leader or church is perfect – it's made up of people. Only our Father in Heaven is perfect. People often become obsessed with finding that alluring church or relationship that offers them the missing 20 percent, but in breaking relationships, they find they only have 20 percent and have left 80 behind.

I have found that in church community, most offense occurs around this – the unknown will of God. You see, you have the known will of God, such as 'don't murder', thanksgiving as part of worship, 'blessed are the meek'. These are clearly communicated wills of God clearly marked out in scripture. But where offense finds a resting place is with the unknown will of God. When will I get married? Is it time to launch my ministry? Should I resign? Is he the one? The moment people hear what they are not ready for, or when leaders do not agree with their interpretation of the unknown will of God, which is subjective at times, offense sets in. Believers, don't fall for this trap. The level of dishonour is too high in the kingdom. This needs to change.

There is a more excellent way to give. There is a more excellent way to serve. There is a more excellent way to worship. There is a more excellent way to preach and teach. There is a more excellent way to do business. There is a more excellent way to speak and conduct relationships - and that more excellent way is honour.

**WE NEED A MORE
EXCELLENT WAY OF OPERATING.**

HONOUR IS THE MORE EXCELLENT WAY.

Conclusion

We have both a spiritual and moral responsibility to ensure that our lives and our walk with God exemplify the coined term "HONOUR". Extensive research has gone into mankind's way of life, in which it establishes traditions both good and bad that has promoted and taught us that our lives are merely a sum of our thoughts. These thoughts that are founded in our imaginations are framed in the cultures of our home and the corridors of the educational institutions which have previously housed some of the greatest of philosophers of times pasts that were bold enough to challenge the status quo by embracing both expert and academic feedback to inform their present reality with a desire for improvement. Whilst this was a very noble characteristic of continuous development, this system has not produced the desired outcomes as predicted and all that was transferred from one generation to another was complex issues that arose in every advancing generation.

The one who created life, Yahweh, and the one who breathes His life into man so that man can live, sets out a course of action for mankind to follow and live by. It's always the imagination of mankind's unregenerate mind that poses a challenge to the advancement of society. It is the way of Jesus Christ that ultimately ensures that the lives of society are ever growing in the knowledge of El Elyon's infinite wisdom.

Let us return to the original design of God's word where our minds are disciplined to stay in the validity and the authenticity of His Word. Honouring this virtue will ultimately align our lives to "as a man thinketh so is he". Let our minds reflect honour, let our walk exemplify honour, let our decisions always resemble honour and let every decision and transition be found in honour.

REFERENCES AND RESEARCH

Merriam Webster Dictionary

Bible: Thomas Nelson New King James version

Bible: New International Version

Strong's Hebrew and Greek Lexicon

Strong's Concordance

Matthew Henry commentary

www.bibleref.com

www.biblehub.com

Book publications

Eckhardt, John. 2009. God still speaks. Charisma media

Strong, James. 2003. Thomas Nelson; Super Value Series edition

Henry, Matthew. 2003 Thomas Nelson, Matthew Henry's Concise Commentary on the Whole Bible (Super Value Series)

Made in the USA
Columbia, SC
03 July 2021

41352914R00046